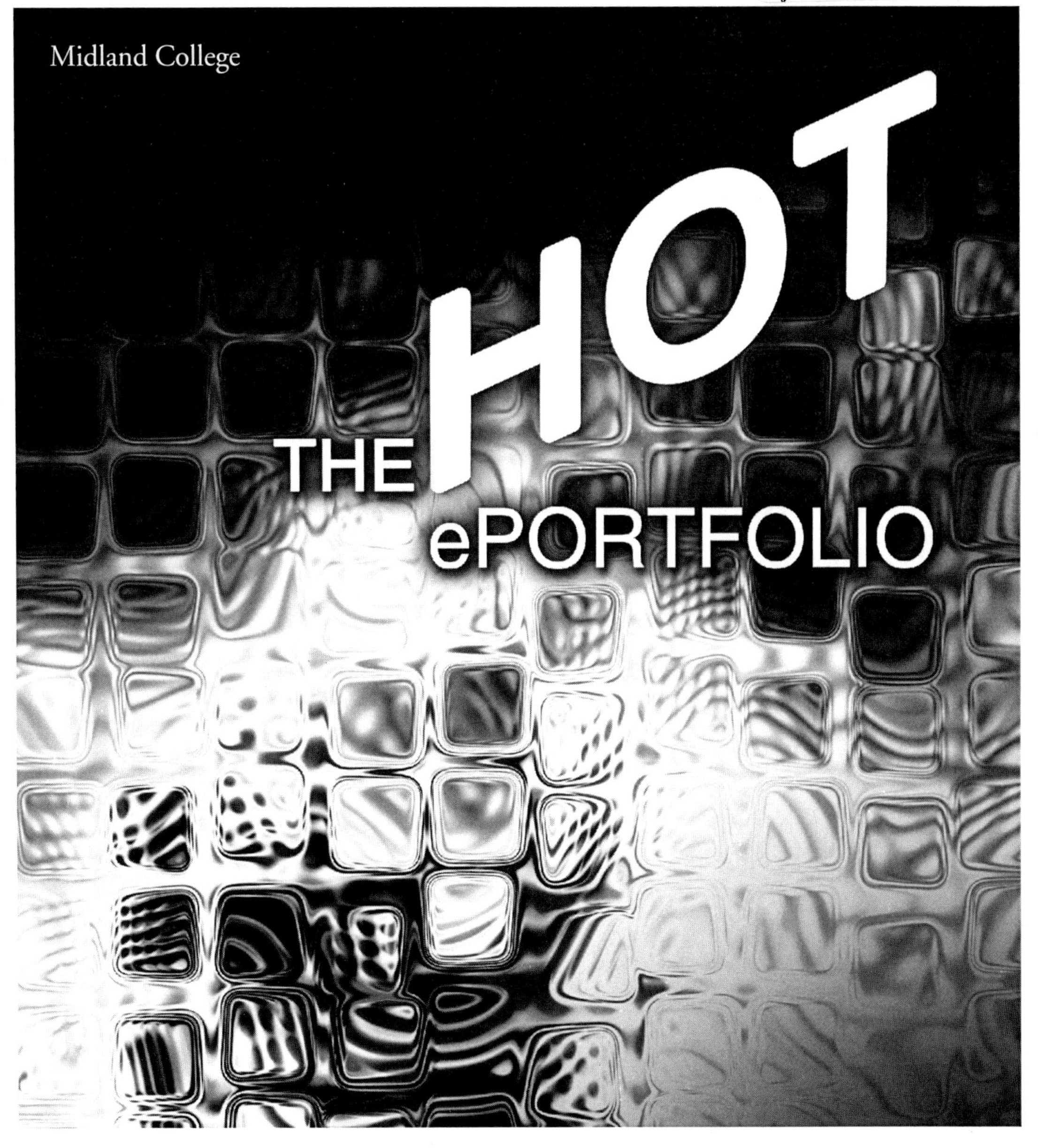

MARY E. BRASELTON, Ed.D.

Cover image © Shutterstock, Inc.

Kendall Hunt
publishing company

www.kendallhunt.com
Send all inquiries to:
4050 Westmark Drive
Dubuque, IA 52004-1840

ISBN 978-0-7575-7705-5

Printed in the United States of America
10 9 8 7 6 5 4 3 2

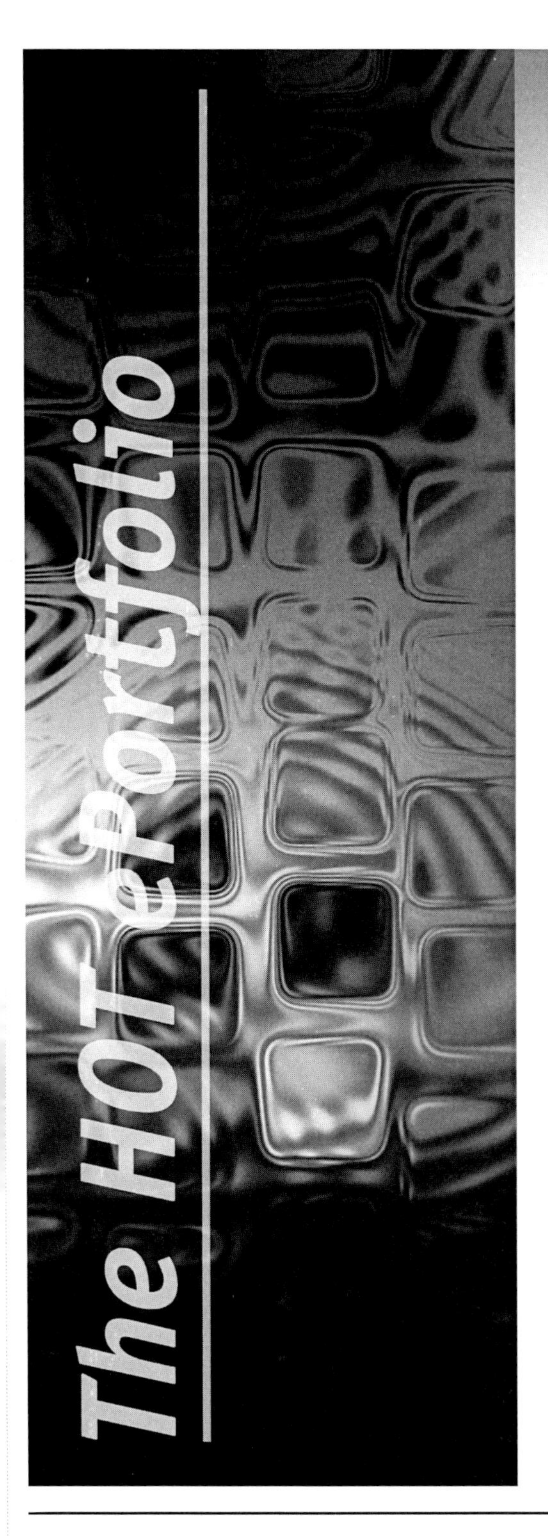

CONTENTS

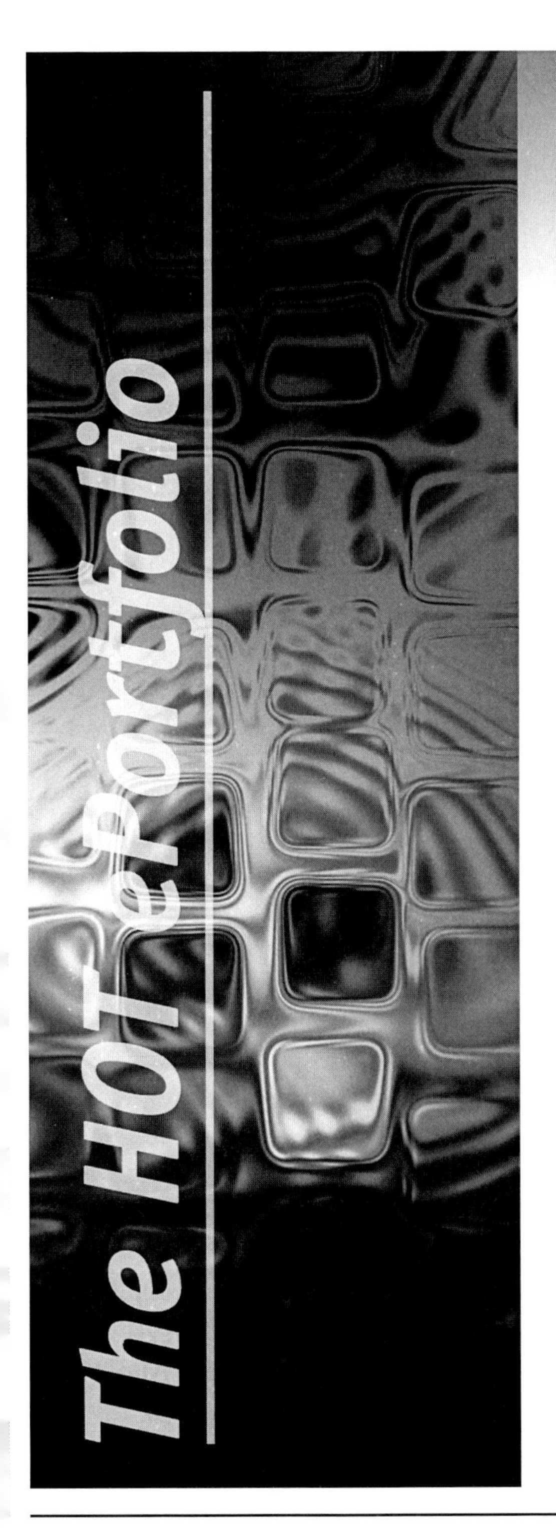

INTRODUCTION to *The HOT ePortfolio*

• • • • • • • • • • • • • • • •

Preparing for the future means learning how to function in a technological society. Children all over the world are interacting with computers at earlier and earlier ages, so it is imperative that teachers not only keep up with the knowledge of their students, but that they also interject technology into their courses in such a way to challenge them.

Why This Book?

- *The HOT ePortfolio* is based on the universal need to engage students in Higher Order Thinking Skills (HOTS).
- *The HOT ePortfolio* challenges students to rely upon their own unique abilities to think through problems to their logical conclusions.
- *The HOT ePortfolio* allows students to interact with course materials and objectives in hands-on activities through technology.
- *The HOT ePortfolio* forces students to practice thinking skills when answers are not "cut and dried".
- *The HOT ePortfolio* results in a tangible product that allows students to reflect upon their own learning.

The ePortfolio Defined

Known as the ePortfolio or the digital portfolio, the electronic portfolio is a way a student can show evidence of learning. Organizationally, ePortfolios are flexible: they may showcase intricate or simple, many or few learning products. The ePortfolio can be created on a small scale and saved on a DVD-RW for ease of storage. On the other hand, and on a much larger scale, many colleges and universities are turning to the digital portfolio, which begins with the first classes a freshman student enrolls in. The portfolio continues to build evidence of learning throughout the college years, documenting and showcasing outstanding academic performance from college entry to graduation, ending in a capstone experience.

THE ePORTFOLIO CONCEPT

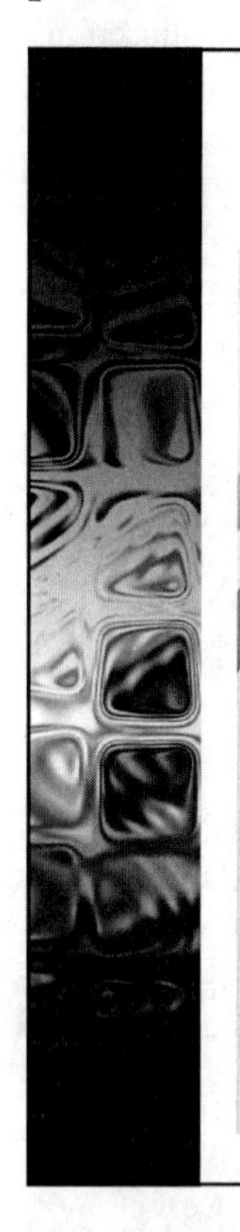

The ePortfolio Concept

- *Different from a traditional container portfolio;*
- *Based on the 4-P model; and*
- *Allows for hands-on approach to state competencies.*

Slide Note: The ePortfolio supercedes the container portfolio, which was often compiled in a plastic crate or several 4″ binders. These portfolios were cumbersome and principals did not want to look at them. The "4-P model" is the problem, process, product, and performance. Because teachers are encouraged to reflect upon every facet of their work, it is appropriate to add an /R/ to the 4-Ps, thus making it 4-P + R.

E-portfolios can be designed for most individual classes—academic, elective, or technology-based. The academic degree any future educator takes requires communication skills (oral and written), problem-solving, project completion, collaboration, organizational skills, performance through curriculum and lesson planning, discipline management plans, student teaching, etc. In short, it is imperative that the preservice teacher demonstrate competency in all of the pedagogical standards which any given state might require and each of the standards incorporates technology to some extent. Beyond demonstrating knowledge of and expertise in the standards themselves, an electronic portfolio demonstrates expertise in technology.

Audience

While this book is primarily intended for preservice teachers, it should be noted that *The HOT ePortfolio* presents a unique form of authentic assessment for most academic courses or subject-specific portfolio. Any teacher or instructor of any course can take the basic premise of this book and apply it to a subject-specific course by substituting the subject-specific objectives and assignments.

The State of Texas and Teacher Education

A recent issue of the *Texas Education News* included statements from an address Texas Education Commissioner, Robert Scott, made to the Texas Association of School Boards/Texas Association of School Administrators. He said, "Texas is taking the first steps toward creating an electronic online 'student portfolio assessment system', that will also include the ability for teachers and students to tap into a broad range of Internet-based news sources, historical documents, and other resources."[1]

The article further names the portfolio system the "ePortfolio", "whereby students can house examples of their work while in high school, college, and beyond."[2]

Four days past the initial speech Commissioner Scott gave, the Texas Education Agency (TEA) requested bids from vendors to provide the digital platform.

Thus, the need for learning about ePortfolios is current and consistent with all future teacher training in Texas. Toward that end, Texas Education Agency consultants provide conferences on the latest trends in classroom technology as applied in the classroom. While all school districts cannot provide financially for the ultimate in computers and technical support, most districts do provide computer labs and perhaps even laptop computers, which students can utilize for creating ePortfolios.

[1] Copyright 2009 by *Texas Education News*, Austin, TX. October 12, 2009. Issue 31.

[2] Ibid.

Teacher Education Programs

The State of Texas urges teacher training programs to integrate technology into each course. The Pedagogy and Professional Responsibilities (PPR) for all levels of teaching (EC-12) have at least one competency which relates to technology.

For example, Competency 9 of the EC-12 PPR states, "The teacher incorporates the effective use of technology to plan, organize, deliver, and evaluate instruction for all students."[3]

Furthermore, the State of Texas specifically charges the technology applications curriculum with the responsibility for technology literacy to meet the No Child Left Behind requirements cited in Title II, Part D.

Technology Applications

"The Technology Applications Unit provides direction and leadership for the Technology Applications curriculum, grades Prekindergarten-12. Technology Applications includes the teaching, learning, and integration of digital technology knowledge and skills across the curriculum, especially in the foundation areas, to support learning and promote student achievement."[4]

Authentic Assessment

A widely-used form of authentic assessment is the course/subject portfolio. *The HOT ePortfolio* text allows students to practice this form of assessment and gain knowledge that will assist in the preparation of a **professional** portfolio. Instruction for *The HOT ePortfolio* for teacher educators includes creating an electronic portfolio, which documents growth in the 13 competencies of the Pedagogy and Professional Responsibilities (PPR) for Texas teachers.

Once completed, *The HOT ePortfolio* contains representative work samples selected from a variety of course assignments. These work samples demonstrate learning and the progress made in understanding the PPR standards.

[3] Copyright by the Texas Education Agency. All rights reserved. http://www.tea.state.tx.us/index.aspx?id=5938&ekfxmen_noscript=1&ekfxmensel=e105c3e3e_620_634.
[4] Retrieved from http://www.tea.state.tx.us/index2.aspx?id=6230&menu_id=2147483665.

BASIC TOOLS/RULES

The HOT ePortfolio

- is created with Microsoft Office PowerPoint (PPT).
- is created using similar rules as a PPT presentation.
- presents personal knowledge and skills related to the PPR standards.
- testifies to academic progress.
- assesses technology skills and competency.

The student will be expected to

- hyperlink slides and sections;
- insert clip art, photos, sounds, music, video;
- scan certificates and graphic organizers;
- scan documented field experiences, and
- save the product on a CD-R with all links active.

The ePortfolio may contain the following or other products demonstrating learning.

Administrator Interviews
Book Reviews
Class Newsletters
Comments & Reflections
Creative Writings
Essays
Inventories
Journal Entries
Learning Styles Assessments
Letters
Observations and Comments
Photographs
Poetry
Posters
Presentations
Problem Statements & Solutions
Reader-response Logs
Recorded Commentary Reports
Reviews
Self-assessment Checklists
Short Stories
Surveys
Teacher Interviews
Video-taped Performances

The Learning Plan, or Planning for the ePortfolio

A Learning Plan is a document (possibly an interactive or online document) that is used to plan learning, usually over an extended period of time.

From Wikipedia, the free encyclopedia
http://en.wikipedia.org/wiki/Learning_Plan
accessed 10/2/10

Another way to envision the construction of the ePortfolio is through a comprehensive learning plan. An instructor's syllabus might generally be thought of as a learning plan, as it contains at least a general description of the assignments which will be necessary to complete the class successfully.

Most instructors lead their students through the syllabus at the beginning of the semester, in hopes that students will see the scope and sequence of the learning that is to follow. By sharing the scope and sequence of the course, the instructor provides an opportunity for all students to plan time and product effectively. Students who take advantage of this opportunity are often successful.

In the case of *The HOT ePortfolio*, the learning plan is relatively easy to accomplish, for it will follow the course objectives.

Suggested Approach to Developing a Learning Plan

The student

- ✓ follows the syllabus to establish a learning plan;
    - lists the course objectives;
    - identifies as many concrete assignments as possible;
    - estimates the time necessary to complete each assignment;
    - lists and locates resources;
- ✓ creates a tentative calendar for the course;
- ✓ identifies areas which call for additional support/help;
- ✓ brainstorms ideas for products/assignments;
- ✓ locates a like-minded individual who will network;
- ✓ conferences with the instructor for additional hints.

These suggestions are flexible and nonlinear, but all are important to organization and planning, two key characteristics of happy teachers.

Portfolio Assessment

Portfolios are extensively used in the field of education as a form of performance or authentic assessment. The portfolio is flexible in that it can be used to show student learning/growth at the end of a unit, a semester, or a year. In the case of university-based portfolios, they can be used as capstone or senior examinations. Students who are not "good test takers" often excel with portfolios because the individual presentation shows more than a predetermined answer to a question, which

may or may not be valid. This form of assessment gives each student multiple opportunities to demonstrate what he knows.

The content of the portfolio can range from structured or open-ended and creative class assignments. Normally, said assignments are collected over a specified amount of time and therefore, are able to show educational growth or maturity in a given discipline.

It is imperative for the instructor to use a predetermined set of standards to guide the student in portfolio preparation and to set up parameters for assessment. A sample grading matrix is provided.

EX=Exceeds Expectations　　M= Meets Expectations
AB=Above Average　　NM = Does not meet expectations

Organization	Student Self-Evaluation				Instructor Evaluation				TOTAL
	EX	AB	M	NM	EX	AB	M	NM	
	90 -100	80 - 89	70 - 79	0 - 69	90 -100	80 - 89	70 - 79	0 - 69	Score
Created appropriate TOC									
Created appropriate subsections for Electronic Portfolio									
Subsections logically organized Readability of pages (font types and sizes (see SOS), color schemes, amount of info).									
Content									
Attached/Linked Resume									
Bulleted page with philosophy statements									
Linked Philosophy (full text)									
4 Scanned/Linked FEX Observation Reports									
Linked/Scanned FEX LOG									
Linked Lesson Plans									
Linked Reflections/13 Competencies									
Linked Scholar's Vocabulary/13 Competencies									
Attached Junior Achievement Journal if applicable									
Attached multimedia presentation									
Demonstrates growth in PPR standard expectations									
Professional Style									
Appropriate content and appearance for professional audience, constructed as portfolio-not presentation									
Major Slides bulleted, linked to full-text documents.									
Clarity and conciseness of written text									
No errors in written text (spelling, punctuation, grammar)									

Comments here and/or on back.

Student Total ________　　Instructor Total ________

Student Average ________　　Instructor Average ________

Constructing *The HOT ePortfolio*

This part of *The HOT ePortfolio* demonstrates a suggested table of contents.

Table of Contents for *The HOT ePortfolio*

The following list contains the outline for *The HOT ePortfolio*. The **boldfaced** headings provide key words taken from each of the 13 EC-12 Pedagogy and Professional Responsibilities test framework. Under each boldfaced heading are key words which succinctly describe the content of the individual competency. For example, key words for competency 1 is *human development*.

Two additional sections indicate the subtopics to be documented within *The HOT ePortfolio*. For example, under *credentials* appears the current resumé, the philosophy of education, etc.

Credentials
- Resumé
- Educational Philosophy
- Degree Plan
- Teacher-Related Activities
- Motivation to Teach

Designing Instruction & Assessment
- Human Development
- Diversity
- How Learning Occurs

Classroom Environment
- Supportive Environment
- Classroom Management

Implementing Instruction
- Communication
- Engaging Instruction
- Technology
- Assessment

Professional Roles & Responsibilities
- Family Communication
- Professional Activities
- Legal & Ethical

APPENDICES
- Reflections

The HOT ePortfolio contains six sections as elaborated above. First, the student creates an initial "shell" for the ePortfolio and adds to it as the term progresses. The "shell" is composed of the master slides including one for each of the 13 competencies. As students complete each assignment, the product is uploaded into the ePortfolio and linked appropriately. In the case of prerequisite courses, the ePortfolio may carry over to a second or third semester.

Constructing *The HOT ePortfolio*

Tips to think about before you start constructing the ePortfolio:

Use a thumb drive to save ALL your work until you are ready to burn it to CD.

- Use PowerPoint 97-2004 to create your portfolio. If you have 2007 on your computer, save everything (all documents, etc.) in the earlier version so they can be read on any computer you use for your student-led conference and your portfolio assessment final.
- Create a **document folder** for your portfolio. Save this PowerPoint (.ppt) as the first document in the folder. Your folder should have these files in it: every document, photo, clip art, etc., that you attach to your portfolio must be in this folder.

DOCUMENT FOLDER:

Documents	ePortfolio PPT
Music File	Video File

- The student will select a design that is appropriate for a **professional** portfolio. Any picture you use must be professional in nature (i.e., no Glamour Shots).
- Periodically open your portfolio on another computer to be sure all hyperlinks work.
- Music or a recording introducing yourself may be added but is not necessary.
- A video introducing yourself and explaining the use of the portfolio may be added but is not necessary.

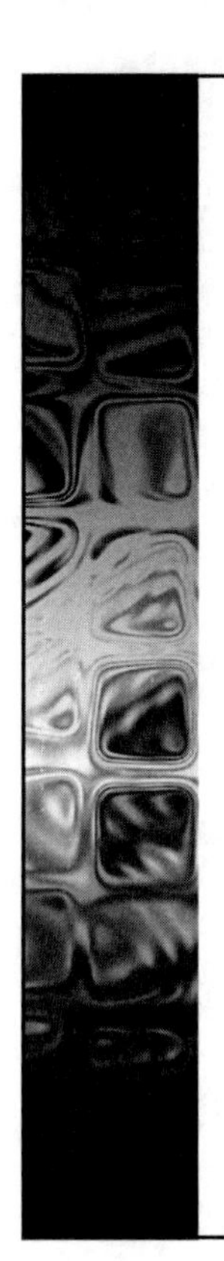

SLIDE 1: TABLE OF CONTENTS

Credentials

Designing Instruction & Assessment

Classroom Environment

Implementing Instruction

Professional Roles & Responsibilities

Appendices

DR. MARY E. BRASELTON

EDUC 1301
Fall Semester, 2011
Instructor

- On the first slide, insert a text box and list the six Table of Contents (TOC) sections as listed on this slide. The credentials section will link to personal information. The remaining four "chapter" titles represent the four domains of the Pedagogy and Professional Development (PPR) standards for beginning teachers. A full text description of the standards can be found at *http://texes.ets.org/assets/pdf/testprep_manuals/160_pedprofrespec_12_55015_web.pdf* (copy/paste) pages 6-16 (10-20). The appendices will include glossaries, reflections, or extra work.
- The Table of Contents section should be arranged following competency order.
- The cover slide must have the student's name, the course, instructor, semester, and year.
- A new slide will be added for each of the sections listed in the TOC. For example, a new slide will be added with the term "Credentials" as a title. The term on this "home" page will be highlighted and a hyperlink will be created taking the viewer to the credentials slide.

This process will be repeated with each of the additional sections.

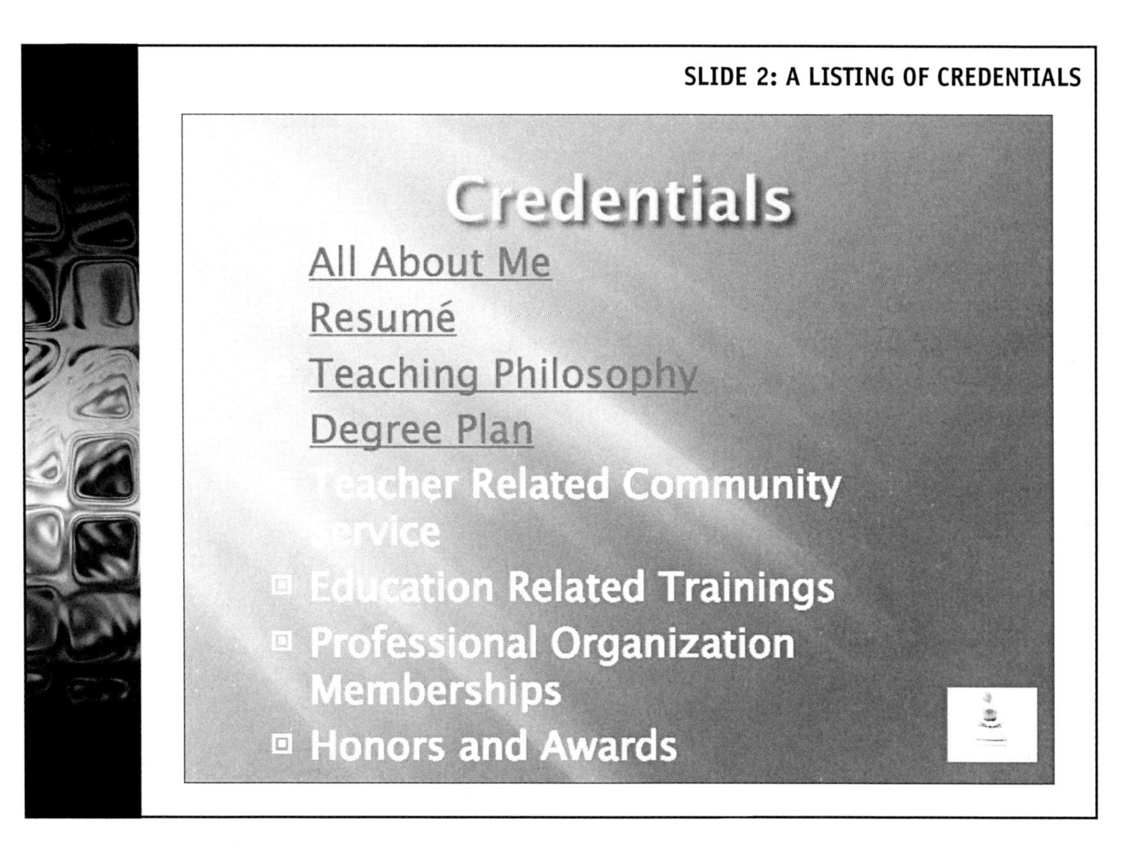

- At the bottom of the slide, the word "Home" or a *symbol* must be added to link back to the Table of Contents.
- The three required entries on this slide are: resumé, teaching philosophy, and degree plan. The others may be added if the student has entries that relate to these areas. Additional areas may be added if appropriate or as instructor directs.
- Always introduce a hyperlinked document with a statement of personal philosophy.
  - Resumé: Students must develop a resumé. The resumé is a Word document saved in the documents file and is hyperlinked to the word *Resumé* on the Credentials slide. Do not put your resumé on a slide. The resumé slide will have a brief statement about your **teaching objective** and a full text link which is hyperlinked.
  - Teaching Philosophy: This phrase is hyperlinked to a slide with the title, Teaching Philosophy. Sample of slide with short philosophy statement + full text link.

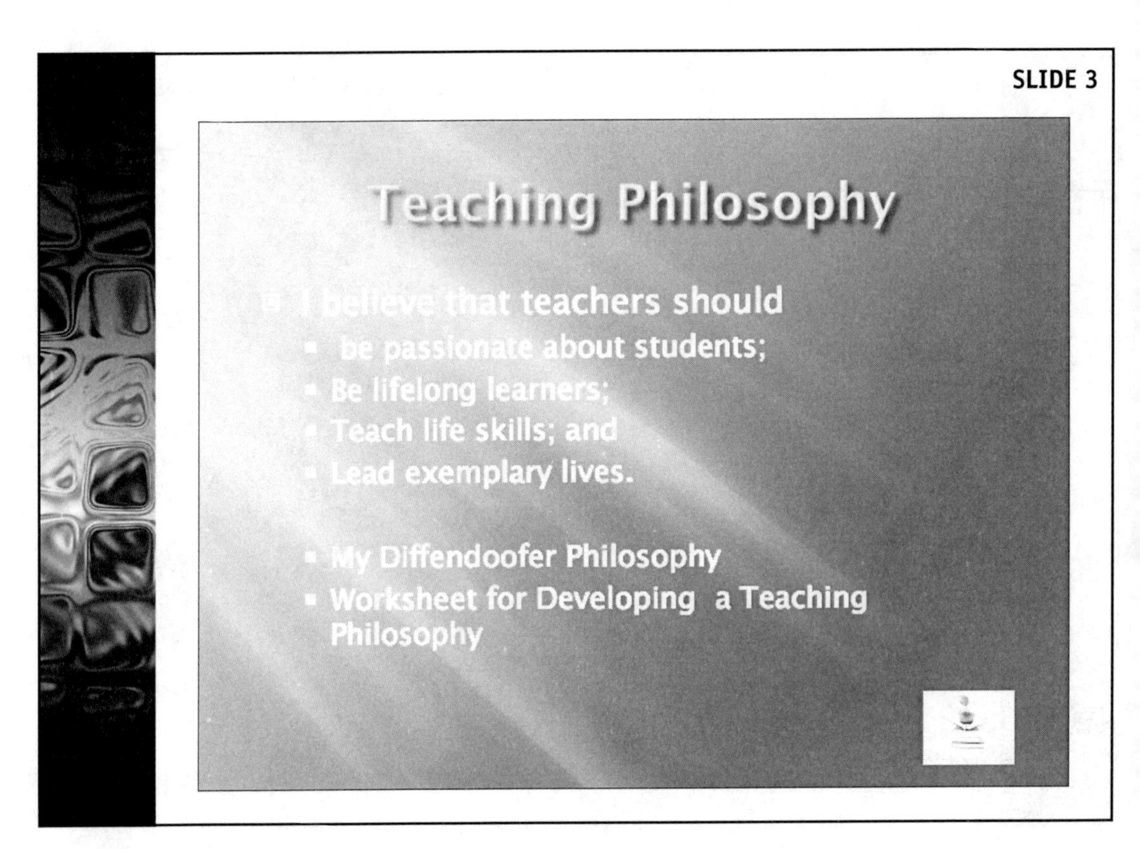

On this slide are 5-6 bullets that simply state in short phrases, elements of the student's teaching philosophy.

Degree Plan: This phrase is hyperlinked to a slide with the title, Degree Plan. Students must make a personal statement that includes the description of the degree plan they are graduating under and when they plan to graduate from Midland College. Photos and/or clip art are optional. If you do not have a copy of your degree plan, see an advisor soon.

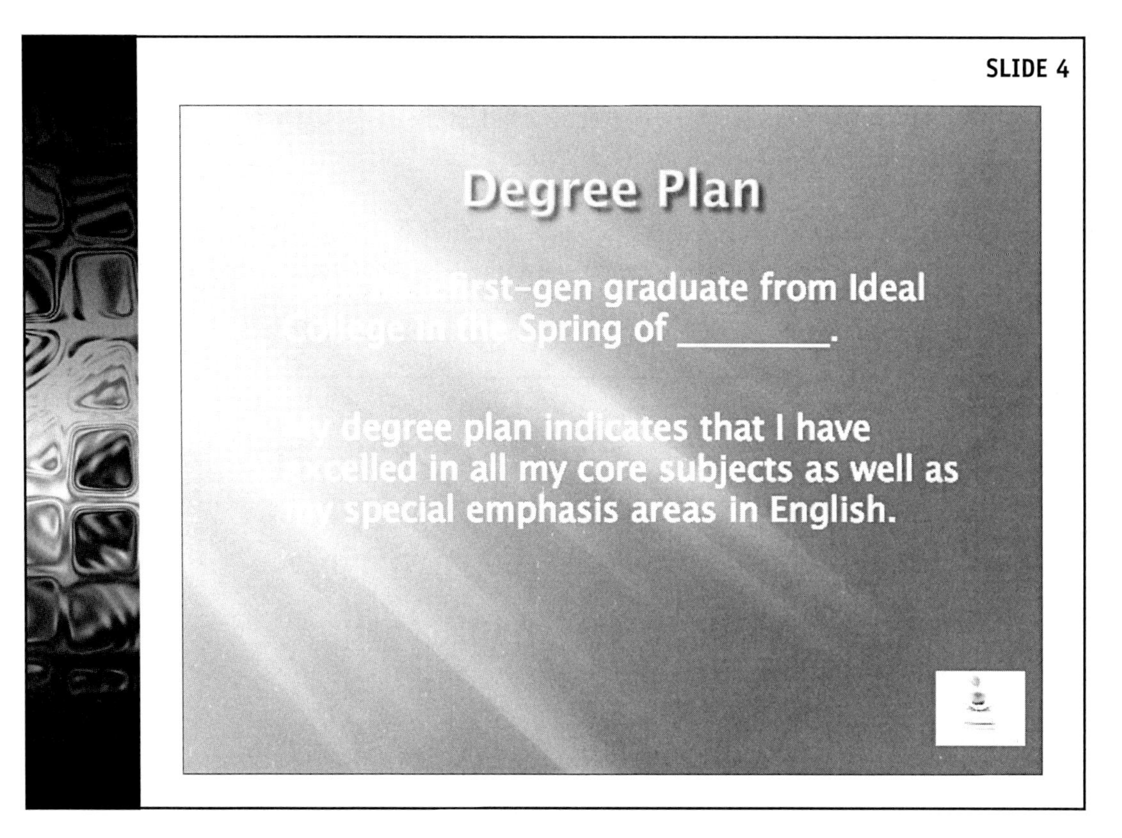

- Test Scores: A student might hyperlink this phrase to entrance scores, or a slide that provides a list of scores on external exams such as SAT, ACT, THEA (only list these scores if they are exceptional).
- Teacher Related Community Service: This phrase is hyperlinked to a slide with the phrase as the title only if the student has completed projects such as a Junior Achievement presenter, Sunday school teacher, 4H project leader, scouting, etc. If a slide is added, students will provide a brief description of the service and may include hyperlinked scanned copies of certificates, awards, photos and/or links to newspaper articles describing the service.
- Education Related Trainings: This phrase is hyperlinked to a slide with the phrase as the title only if the student has completed workshops or training that relates to being a teacher of children. Technology trainings and courses may be included in this section if it applies to integrating technology into the teaching and learning process. Students may also include First Aid training certificates and things of that nature.
- Professional Organization Memberships: This phrase is hyperlinked to a slide with the phrase as the title only if the student has joined and is/has participated in educator-related professional clubs, groups, or organizations. On this slide, students might list their affiliations.

If the student has been actively involved, there may be additional slides with more information such as activities coordinated, presentations made, offices held, etc.

- Honors and Awards: Students may hyperlink a slide indicating their recognition in any area, examples might be MVP for a sport, Who's Who, Dean's List, etc.

After establishing one's credentials, the first of the four Standards of the Pedagogy and Professional Responsibilities is documented. The first slide will contain key wording for the Standard and the four competencies (key words) developed under this Standard:

FIRST Standard Slide with four Competencies listed.

- This is the cover slide for the portfolio "chapter" addressing Standard 1 of the Texas Pedagogy and Professional Responsibilities for beginning teachers. This Standard covers topics related to designing instruction and assessment. Key Words for the first four competencies are listed on this slide.
- A new slide will be added, hyperlinked, for each of these competencies on which a student will write a brief philosophy of their understanding of knowledge the competency requires.

- The philosophy must include opinions and examples relating to one or more of the concepts addressed in the competency.
- Class assignments or products from individual efforts that demonstrate the understanding of the competency should be hyperlinked to the competency. There should always be a statement introducing a hyperlinked document.

Example of statement and hyperlink of a student-initiated learning:
"I wanted to know more about the cognitive development of children and searched the Internet for the concept. I enjoyed watching Piaget and other resources *(Piaget is hyperlinked to the YouTube video with him discussing his theory of cognitive development).* To help me understand Piaget, I created a pictorial version of Piaget's Stages of Development in the linked document entitled Piaget and the Comics."

IMPORTANT: The "home" symbol should be hyperlinked to the initial cover page of the portfolio. On each of the slides related to this competency, the same symbol should be hyperlinked to the "chapter" cover slide. There is no need to insert the symbol on an attachment, when the window is closed, the viewer is taken back to the slide with the hyperlink.

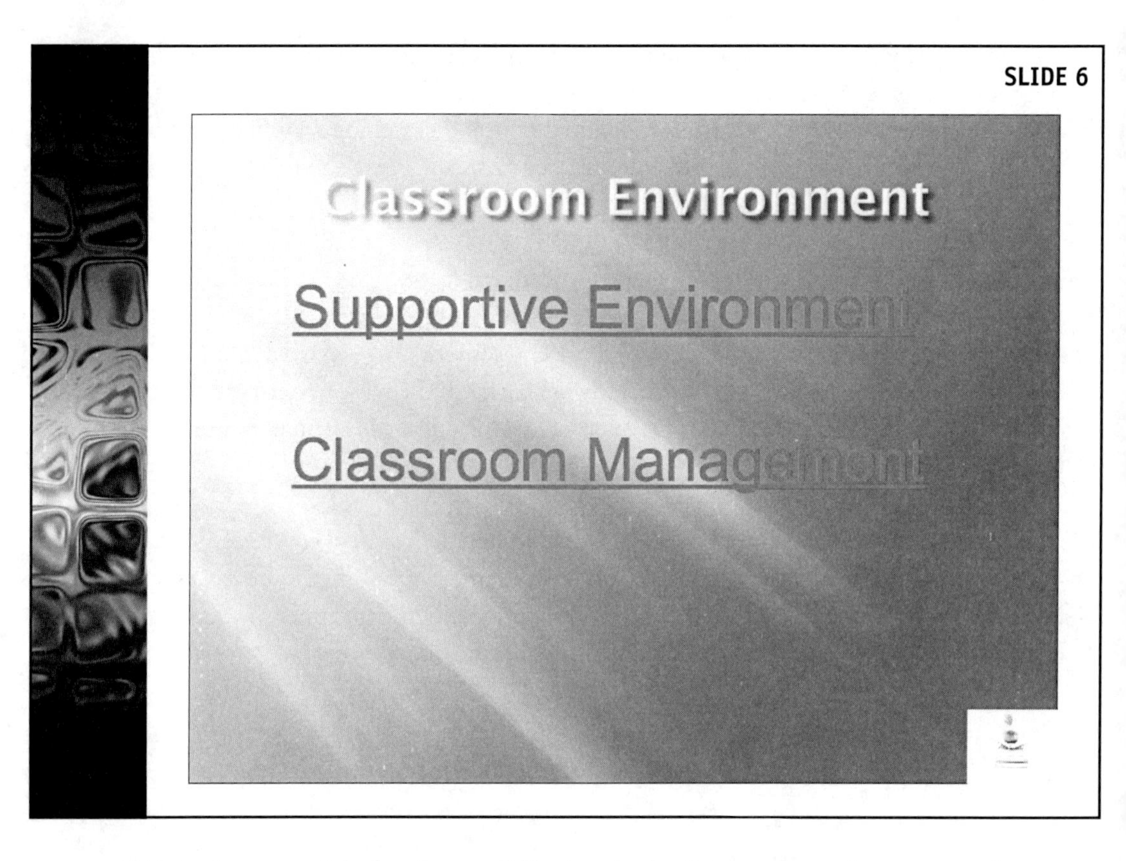

This is the cover slide for the portfolio Standard 2 "chapter" on classroom environment. PPR Competencies 5 and 6 are listed on this slide. As you can see, this part of the PPT is developed the same as Standard 1.

- A new slide will be added and hyperlinked, for each of these competencies on which a student will write a statement of understanding of the competency requirements.

- Class assignments or products from individual efforts that demonstrate the understanding of the competency should be hyperlinked. There should always be a statement introducing a hyperlinked document.

- The "home" symbol should be hyperlinked to the initial cover page of the portfolio. On each of the slides related to this competency, the symbol should be hyperlinked to the "chapter" cover slide. There is no need to insert the symbol on an attachment, when the window is closed, the viewer is taken back to the slide with the hyperlink.

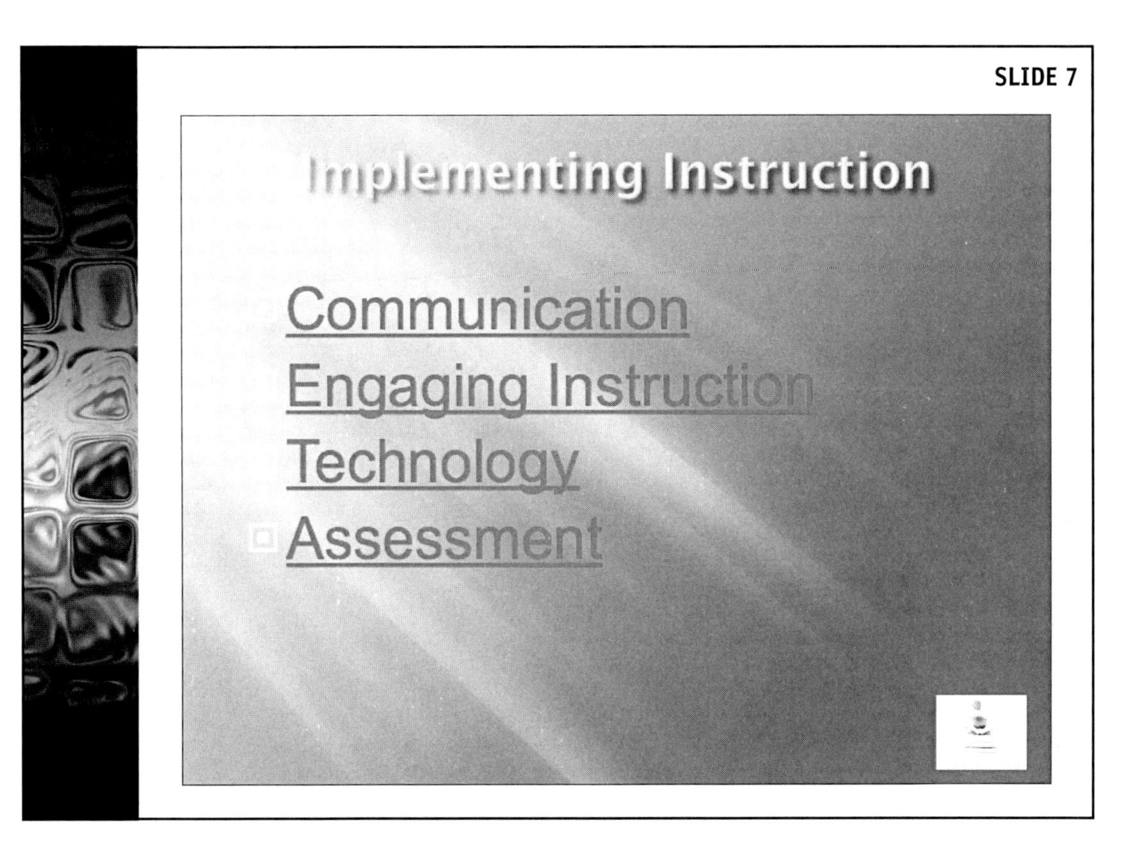

This is the cover slide for the portfolio Standard 3 "chapter" on implementing instruction. PPR Competencies 7, 8, 9, and 10 are listed on this slide.

- A new slide will be added and hyperlinked, for each of these competencies on which a student will write a statement of understanding of the competency requirements.
- The paragraph must include opinions and examples relating to one or more of the concepts addressed in the competency.
- If there are class assignments or products from individual efforts that demonstrate the understanding of the competency, it should be hyperlinked. There should always be a statement introducing a hyperlinked document.
- The "home" symbol should be hyperlinked to the initial cover page of the portfolio. On each of the slides related to this competency, the symbol should be hyperlinked to the "chapter" cover slide. There is no need to insert the symbol on an attachment, when the window is closed, the viewer is taken back to the slide with the hyperlink.

This is the cover slide for the portfolio Standard 4 "chapter" on professional roles and responsibilities. PPR competencies 11, 12, and 13 are listed on this slide.

- A new slide will be added and hyperlinked, for each of these competencies on which a student will write a statement of understanding of what the competency requires.
- Class assignments or products from individual efforts that demonstrate the understanding of the competency should be hyperlinked. There should always be a statement introducing a hyperlinked document.
- The "home" symbol should be hyperlinked to the initial cover page of the portfolio. On each of the slides related to this competency, the symbol should be hyperlinked to the "chapter" cover slide. There is no need to insert the symbol on an attachment, when the window is closed, the viewer is taken back to the slide with the hyperlink.

The final listing in the Table of Contents is the APPENDICES. As with the other divider slides, this one will list what is included in the appendices. Each of the items in the list will be hyperlinked to the document. Include a "home" icon on the bottom of this slide.

APPENDICES	
Glossary	Home
Reflections	
Research	

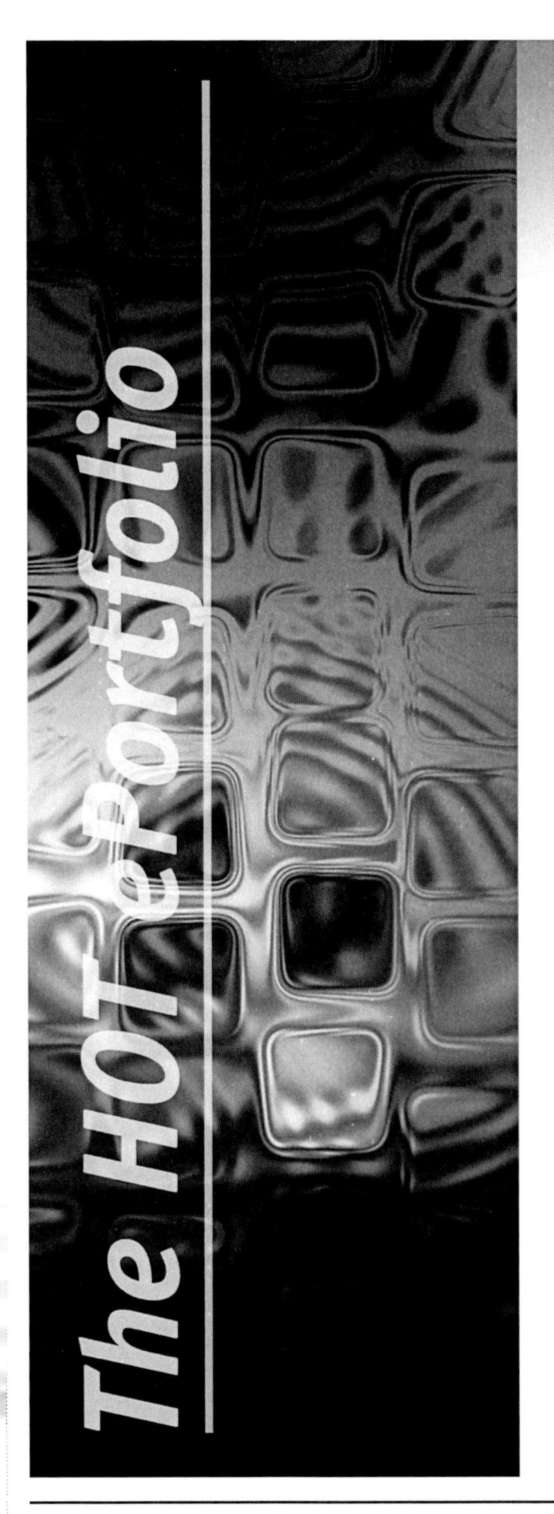

THE INTERACTIVE CD

Fewer things are harder to put up with than the annoyance of a good example.

- Mark Twain

Mark Twain's quote is intended to be humorous; still, most of us can benefit by having good examples—especially, when we are asked to create something that we have never done before.The model ePortfolio on the CD contains various assignments (rather than products) made in the Introduction to Education class. Each of the ePortfolios contain various assignments and products from the Introduction to Education. The intent of the ePortfolio is to begin the portfolio in the Introduction class and to add to and refine the portfolio in subsequent classes.

Some students enter the Introduction to Education class having never created a PPT presentation, then some, enter class with a host of technology skills. Either way, creating a *professional* portfolio takes new knowledge and a great deal of thinking—that is why it is called *The HOT ePortfolio*. Good luck in all your imaginings!

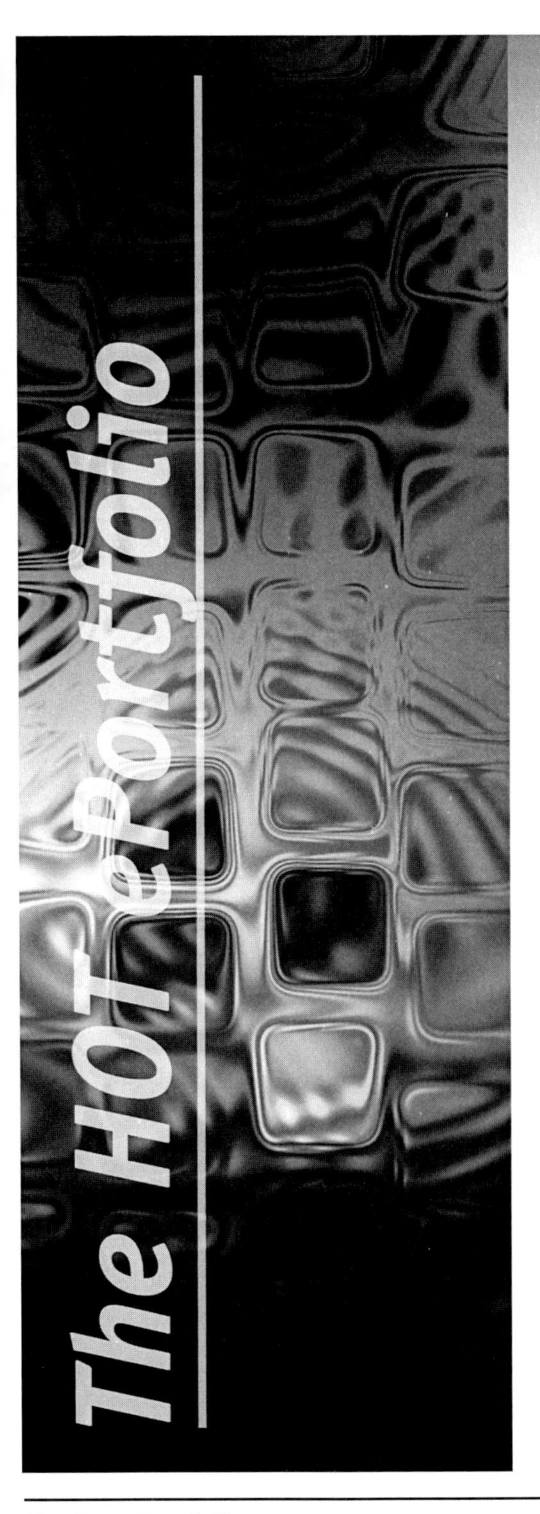

ABOUT THE AUTHOR

Dr. Mary E. Braselton is an Associate Professor of Education and Director of the Associate of Arts degree at Midland College, Midland, Texas. She holds an undergraduate degree from the University of Texas at Austin, a Master's and post-bacc work from West Texas A&M University at Canyon, Texas, and a doctorate from Texas Tech University in Lubbock, Texas.

She has over 28 years of experience teaching high school, community college, and university students. Her teaching experience includes English, Speech Communications, Classroom Management, Pedagogy, Reading in the Secondary Content Areas, and Educational Psychology.

Dr. Braselton's research interests include higher education on the Llano Estacado, Teacher Voice, and all subjects relevant to the successful training of teachers. She has published in excess of 35 articles, textbook chapters, a textbook, and chaired numerous grants related to teacher education. She is currently spearing an initiative to organize the West Texas Community College Consortium for Teacher Education Programs (WTC3TEP).

As an avid supporter of Kappa Delta Pi an International Honor Society for Education, Dr. Braselton strongly supports student organizations which promote professional growth.